W9-BWU-430

202 Mamaroneck Avenue
White Plains, NY 10601
ISBN 0-88088-426-6
Library of Congress No. 89-63623
Printed in Hong Kong
5

CONTENTS

THANK YOU, IN GRATITUDE AND GLADNESS

Be glad of life because it gives you the chance to love and to work and to play and to look up at the stars.

HENRY VAN DYKE

When eating bamboo sprouts, remember the man who planted them.

CHINESE PROVERB

Is it so small a thing to have enjoyed the sun, to have lived light in the spring, to have loved, to have thought, to have done?

MATTHEW ARNOLD

Praise the ripe field, not the green corn.

IRISH PROVERB

I will tell you, scholar, I have heard a grave divine say that God has two dwellings, one in heaven, and the other in a meek and thankful heart.

IZAAK WALTON

Every blade of grass has its share of the dews of heaven.

PROVERB

No one is as capable of gratitude as one who has emerged from the kingdom of night.

ELIE WIESEL

He is a wise man who does not grieve for the things which he has not, but rejoices for those which he has.

EPICTETUS

Nothing is worth more than this day.

GOETHE

What I saw was equal ecstasy:
One universal smile it seemed of all things.

DANTE

Gratitude takes three forms: a feeling in the heart, an expression in words, and a giving in return.

PROVERB

He enjoys much who is thankful for little; a grateful mind is both a great and a happy mind.

THOMAS SECKER

The world is a fine place and worth fighting for.

ERNEST HEMINGWAY

Gratitude is one of the least articulate of the emotions, especially when it is deep.

FELIX FRANKFURTER

Gratitude preserves old friendships, and procures new.

PROVERB

I will give thanks unto thee, for I am fearfully and wonderfully made.

PSALM 139, VERSE 14

For this relief much thanks.

SHAKESPEARE,
Hamlet

How far that little candle throws his beams!
So shines a good deed in a naughty world.

SHAKESPEARE

A joyful and pleasant thing it is to be thankful.

PRAYER BOOK

I am not afraid of tomorrow for I have seen yesterday and I love today.

WILLIAM ALLEN WHITE

The mere sense of living is joy enough.

EMILY DICKINSON

In this world of sin and sorrow there is always something to be thankful for; as for me, I rejoice that I am not a Republican.

H. L. MENCKEN

When I find a great deal of gratitude in a poor man, I take it for granted there would be as much generosity if he were rich.

ALEXANDER POPE

I would maintain that thanks are the highest form of thought; and that gratitude is happiness doubled by wonder.

G. K. CHESTERTON

Gratitude is a fruit of great cultivation; you do not find it among gross people.

SAMUEL JOHNSON

Gratitude is the memory of the heart.

J. B. MASSIEU

Love has no other desire but to fulfill itself. To melt and be like a running brook that sings its melody to the night. To wake at dawn with a winged heart and give thanks for another day of loving.

KAHLIL GIBRAN

One can never pay in gratitude; one can only pay "in kind" somewhere else in life.

ANNE MORROW LINDBERGH

The greatest wealth is contentment with a little.

PROVERB

Two kinds of gratitude: the sudden kind We feel for what we take, the larger kind We feel for what we give.

EDWIN ARLINGTON ROBINSON

And only when we are no longer afraid do we begin to live in every experience, painful or joyous; to live in gratitude for every moment, to live abundantly.

DOROTHY THOMPSON

Thanksgiving comes to us out of the prehistoric dimness, universal to all ages and all faiths. At whatever straws we must grasp, there is always a time for gratitude and new beginnings.

J. ROBERT MOSKIN

There is as much greatness of mind in acknowledging a good turn as in doing it.

SENECA

A good wife and health are a man's best wealth.

PROVERB

There are no riches above a sound body, and no joy above the joy of the heart.

PROVERB

Contentment is the philosopher's stone, which turns all it toucheth into gold; the poor man is rich with it, the rich man poor without it.

PROVERB

The gown is hers that wears it, and the world is his that enjoys it.

PROVERB

Believe that life is worth living and your belief will help create the fact.

WILLIAM JAMES

THANK YOU FOR LOVE AND HAPPINESS

What a wonderful life I've had! I only wish I'd realized it sooner.

COLETTE

Whoever is happy will make others happy too. He who has courage and faith will never perish in misery.

ANN FRANK

Love doesn't make the world go 'round. Love is what makes the ride worthwhile.

FRANKLIN P. JONES

Be not too critical of others, and love much.

ALDOUS HUXLEY'S MOTHER
to her son

He only lives who living enjoys life.

MENANDER

Joys are our wings.

JEAN PAUL RICHTER

Butterflies are colorful and bright and gentle and have no way to harm you. They go about their business and bring others pleasure while doing it, because just seeing one flying around makes people happy. I'd like to think of myself as bringing people happiness while I do my business, which is my music. I'm content with what I am, and butterflies seem to be content to be just what they are, too. They're gentle, but determined.

DOLLY PARTON

If man is moderate and contented, then even age is no burden; if he is not, then even youth is full of cares.

PLATO

I suppose—the moments one most enjoys are moments—alone—when one unexpectedly stretches something inside you that needs stretching.

GEORGIA O'KEEFFE

It takes life to love life.

EDGAR LEE MASTERS

Love from one being to another can only be that two solitudes come nearer, recognize and protect and comfort each other.

HAN SUYIN

Happiness resides not in possessions and not in gold; the feeling of happiness dwells in the soul.

DEMOCRITUS

Whoever loves much, does much.

THOMAS À KEMPIS

Very little is needed to make a happy life. It is all within yourself, in your way of thinking.

MARCUS AURELIUS

Men can only be happy when they do not assume that the object of life is happiness.

GEORGE ORWELL

Happiness is good health and a bad memory.

INGRID BERGMAN

Be happy. It's one way of being wise.

COLETTE

Happiness is not a state to arrive at, but a manner of traveling.

MARGARET LEE RUNBECK

To love is to place our happiness in the happiness of another.

G. W. VON LEIBNITZ

The sense of existence is the greatest happiness.

BENJAMIN DISRAELI

Him that I love, I wish to be free—even from me.

ANNE MORROW LINDBERGH

Where love is concerned, too much is not ever enough.

PIERRE-AUGUSTIN CARON DE BEAUMARCHAIS

So often when we say "I love you" we say it with a huge "I" and a small "you."

ANTONY,
Russian Orthodox Archbishop of England

The happiest part of a man's life is what he passes lying awake in bed in the morning.

SAMUEL JOHNSON

Happiness is an inside job.

FATHER OF H. JACKSON BROWN, JR.

'Tis better to have loved and lost,
Than never to have loved at all.

ALFRED LORD TENNYSON

Love is not a matter of counting the years; it's making the years count.

WILLIAM SMITH

Happiness is a stock that doubles in a year.
IRA U. COBLEIGH

We can only learn to love by loving.
IRIS MURDOCH

When you reach the heart of life you shall find beauty in all things.
KAHLIL GIBRAN

To enjoy a lifetime romance—fall in love with yourself.
PROVERB

The supreme happiness of life is the conviction of being loved for yourself, or, more correctly, being loved in spite of yourself.

VICTOR HUGO

We can do no great things—only small things with great love.

MOTHER TERESA

When you really want love you will find it waiting for you.

OSCAR WILDE

When Silence speaks for Love, she has much to say.

RICHARD GARNETT

All happiness depends on a leisurely breakfast.

JOHN GUNTHER

Any time that is not spent on love is wasted.

TASSO

But one of the attributes of love, like art, is to bring harmony and order out of chaos.

MOLLY HASKELL

If only we'd stop trying to be happy, we could have a pretty good time.

EDITH WHARTON

Happiness is a perfume you can not pour on others without getting a few drops on yourself.

RALPH WALDO EMERSON

Write it on your heart that every day is the best day in the year.

RALPH WALDO EMERSON

A happy life is one spent learning, earning and yearning.

LILLIAN GISH

The best way to secure future happiness is to be as happy as is rightfully possible to-day.

CHARLES W. ELIOT

'Tis a good thing to laugh at any rate; and if a straw can tickle a man, it is an instrument of happiness.

DRYDEN

What everyone wants from life is continuous and genuine happiness. Happiness is the rational understanding of life and the world.

BARUCH SPINOZA

Love and joy are twins, or born of each other.

HAZLITT

Life itself is the proper binge.

JULIA CHILD

He who defends with love will be secure;
Heaven will save him, and protect him with love.

LAO-TZU

To fill the hour—that is happiness; to fill the hour, and leave no crevice for a repentance or an approval.

RALPH WALDO EMERSON

Happiness lies in the taste, and not in the things; and it is from having what we desire that we are happy—not from having what others think desirable.

DUC DE LA ROCHEFOUCAULD

Hell is yourself [and the only redemption is] when a person puts himself aside to feel deeply for another person.

TENNESSEE WILLIAMS

Happiness makes up in height for what it lacks in length.

ROBERT FROST

The secret of happiness is this: Let your interests be as wide as possible, and let your reactions to the things and persons that interest you be as far as possible friendly rather than hostile.

BERTRAND RUSSELL

. . . the unity that binds us all together, that makes this earth a family, and all men brothers and the sons of God, is love.

THOMAS WOLFE

The moments of happiness we enjoy take us by surprise. It is not that we seize them, but that they seize us.

ASHLEY MONTAGU

There is no soul that does not respond to love, for the soul of man is a guest that has gone hungry these centuries back.

MAURICE MAETERLINCK

Happiness sneaks in through a door you didn't know you left open.

JOHN BARRYMORE

The belief that youth is the happiest time of life is founded on a fallacy. The happiest person is the person who thinks the most interesting thoughts, and we grow happier as we grow older.

WILLIAM LYON PHELPS

A loving heart is the truest wisdom.

CHARLES DICKENS

The happy do not believe in miracles.

JOHANN W. VON GOETHE

Happiness grows at our own firesides, and is not to be picked in strangers' gardens.

DOUGLAS JERROLD

Remember this—that very little is needed to make a happy life.

MARCUS AURELIUS

We are all born for love. It is the principle of existence, and its only end.

BENJAMIN DISRAELI

HOW DO I LOVE THEE?

How do I love thee? Let me count the ways.
I love thee to the depth and breadth and
height
My soul can reach, when feeling out of sight
For the ends of Being and ideal Grace.
I love thee to the level of every day's
Most quiet need, by sun and candlelight.
I love thee freely, as men strive for Right;
I love thee purely, as they turn from
Praise.
I love thee with the passion put to use
In my old griefs, and with my childhood's
faith.
I love thee with a love I seemed to lose
With my lost saints,—I love thee with the
breath,
Smiles, tears, of all my life!—and, if God
choose,
I shall but love thee better after death.

Elizabeth Barrett Browning

GATHER YE ROSEBUDS

Gather ye rosebuds while ye may,
  Old Time is still a-flying;
And this same flower that smiles today
  Tomorrow will be dying.

The glorious lamp of heaven, the Sun,
  The higher he's a-getting,
The sooner will his race be run,
  And nearer he's to setting.

That age is best, which is the first,
  When youth and blood are warmer
But being spent, the worse, and worst
  Times still succeed the former.

Then be not coy, but use your time,
  And while you may, go marry:
For having lost but once your prime,
  You may for ever tarry.

ROBERT HERRICK

ONE-AND-TWENTY

When I was one-and-twenty
  I heard a wise man say,
"Give crowns and pounds and guineas
  But not your heart away;
Give pearls away and rubies
  But keep your fancy free."
But I was one-and-twenty,
  No use to talk to me.
When I was one-and-twenty
  I heard him say again,
"The heart out of the bosom
  Was never given in vain;
'Tis paid with sighs a-plenty
  And sold for endless rue."
And I am two-and-twenty,
  And oh, 'tis true, 'tis true!

A. E. HOUSMAN

THANK YOU FOR FAMILY

The most important thing a father can do for his children is to love their mother.

THEODORE M. HESBURGH

To show a child what has once delighted you, to find the child's delight added to your own, so that there is now a double delight seen in the glow of trust and affection. This is happiness.

J. B. PRIESTLEY

Kinship is healing; we are physicians to each other.

OLIVER SACKS

To each other, we were as normal and nice as the smell of bread. We were just a family. In a family even exaggerations make perfect sense.

JOHN IRVING

A friend loves you for your intelligence, a mistress for your charm, but your family's love is unreasoning; you were born into it and are of its flesh and blood. Nevertheless it can irritate you more than any group of people in the world.

André Maurois

The family [is] the first essential cell of human society.

Pope John XXIII

Family faces are magic mirrors. Looking at people who belong to us, we see the past, present and future.

Gail Lumet Buckley

There's a time when you have to explain to your children why they're born, and it's a marvelous thing if you know the reason by then.

Hazel Scott

Love is staying up all night with a sick child or a healthy adult.

DAVID FROST

Back of every achievement is a proud wife and a surprised mother-in-law.

BROOKS HAYS

No man can possibly know what life means, what the world means, what anything means, until he has a child and loves it. And then the whole universe changes and nothing will ever again seem exactly as it seemed before.

LAFCADIO HEARN

Loving a child doesn't mean giving in to all his whims; to love him is to bring out the best in him, to teach him to love what is difficult.

NADIA BOULANGER

THANK YOU FOR YOUR KINDNESS

Wise sayings often fall on barren ground; but a kind word is never thrown away.

SIR ARTHUR HELPS

If I can stop one heart from breaking,
  I shall not live in vain;
If I can ease one life the aching,
  Or cool one pain,
Or help one fainting robin
  Unto his nest again,
  I shall not live in vain.

EMILY DICKINSON

Kindness in words creates confidence.
Kindness in thinking creates profoundness.
Kindness in giving creates love.

LAO-TZU

Real generosity is doing something nice for someone who'll never find it out.

FRANK A. CLARK

The best portion of a good man's life—
His little, nameless, unremembered acts
Of kindness and love.

WILLIAM WORDSWORTH

Do not keep the alabaster boxes of your love and tenderness sealed up until your friends are dead. Fill their lives with sweetness. Speak approving cheering words while their ears can hear them and while their hearts can be thrilled by them.

GEORGE W. CHILDS

One of the most difficult things to give away is kindness, for it is usually returned.

ANONYMOUS

Whoever gives a small coin to a poor man has six blessings bestowed upon him, but he who speaks a kind word to him obtains eleven blessings.

TALMUD

Give what you have. To some one, it may be better than you dare to think.

HENRY WADSWORTH LONGFELLOW

Good thoughts, even if they are forgotten, do not perish.

PUBLILIUS SYRUS

The best cure for worry, depression, melancholy, brooding, is to sally deliberately forth and try to lift with one's sympathy the gloom of somebody else.

ARNOLD BENNETT

What do we live for, if it is not to make life less difficult for each other?

George Eliot

If a man be gracious to strangers, it shows that he is a citizen of the world, and his heart is no island, cut off from other islands, but a continent that joins them.

Francis Bacon

Rule by kindness rather than fear.

Sallust

Freely ye have received; freely give.

Matthew 10:8

You cannot do a kindness too soon, because you never know how soon it will be too late.

PROVERB

Life is short. Let us make haste to be kind.

HENRI AMIEL

Silver and gold have I none; but such as I have give I thee.

ACTS 3:6

A kind heart is a fountain of gladness, making everything in its vicinity freshen into smiles.

WASHINGTON IRVING

A word of kindness is better than a fat pie.

RUSSIAN PROVERB

He was so benevolent, so merciful a man that he would have held an umbrella over a duck in a shower of rain.

DOUGLAS JERROLD

It is more blessed to give than to receive.

ACTS 3:6

Kindness gives birth to kindness.

SOPHOCLES

The cheapest of all things is kindness, its exercise requiring the least possible trouble and self-sacrifice.

SAMUEL SMILES

To cultivate kindness is a valuable part of the business of life.

SAMUEL JOHNSON

Kindness consists in loving people more than they deserve.

JOUBERT

The only gift is a portion of yourself. The gift without the giver is bare.

JAMES RUSSELL LOWELL

Life is mostly froth and bubble,
  Two things stand like stone,
Kindness in another's trouble,
  Courage in your own.

ADAM LINDSAY GORDON

When I give I give myself.

WALT WHITMAN

THANK YOU FOR BEING A FRIEND

A real friend is one who walks in when the rest of the world walks out.

WALTER WINCHELL

When friends ask, there is no tomorrow.

PROVERB

"Stay" is a charming word in a friend's vocabulary.

AMOS BRONSON ALCOTT

Friendship will not stand the strain of very much good advice for very long.

ROBERT LYND

No man is wise enough by himself.

PLAUTUS

The man who treasures his friends is usually solid gold himself.

MARJORIE HOLMES

Laughter is not a bad beginning for a friendship, and it is the best ending for one.

OSCAR WILDE

Friendship is almost always the union of a part of one mind with a part of another: People are friends in spots.

GEORGE SANTAYANA

Love is a sudden blaze, which soon decays;
Friendship is like the sun's eternal rays;
Not daily benefits exhaust the flame;
It still is giving, and still burns the same.

JOHN GAY

Hold a true friend with both hands.

NIGERIAN PROVERB

Of course platonic friendship is possible—
but only between husband and wife.

ANONYMOUS

A home-made friend wears longer than one
you buy in the market.

AUSTIN O'MALLEY

Friends are like melons; shall I tell you why?
To find one good you must a hundred try.

CLAUDE MERMET

True friends are those seeking solitude together.

ABEL BONNARD

I always felt that the great high privilege, relief and comfort of friendship was that one had to explain nothing.

KATHERINE MANSFIELD

Treat your friends as you do your pictures, and place them in their best light.

JENNIE JEROME CHURCHILL

Change your pleasure, but never change your friends.

VOLTAIRE

There are three faithful friends: an old wife, an old dog, and ready money.

BENJAMIN FRANKLIN

Friendship is like money, easier made than kept.

SAMUEL BUTLER

Friends should be preferred to kings.

VOLTAIRE

Friendship is a plant of slow growth, and must undergo and withstand the shocks of adversity before it is entitled to the appellation.

GEORGE WASHINGTON

The truth is friendship is to me every bit as sacred and eternal as marriage.

KATHERINE MANSFIELD

Always, Sir, set a high value on spontaneous kindness. He whose inclination prompts him to cultivate your friendship of his own accord, will love you more than one whom you have been at pains to attach to you.

SAMUEL JOHNSON

Do not save your loving speeches
For your friends till they are dead;
Do not write them on their tombstones,
Speak them rather now instead.

ANNA CUMMINS

To your good health, old friend,
may you live for a thousand years,
and I be there to count them.

ROBERT SMITH SURTEES

[A friend is] one who is willing to endorse your banknote. Laying down one's life is nothing in comparison.

GAMALIEL BRADFORD

A friend is a present you give yourself.

ROBERT LOUIS STEVENSON

Friendship is the shadow of the evening, which strengthens with the setting sun of life.

JEAN DE LA FONTAINE

A faithful friend is the medicine of life.

APOCRYPHA: ECCLESIASTICUS, VI, 16

Grief can take care of itself, but to get the full value of a joy you must have somebody to divide it with.

MARK TWAIN

The feeling of friendship is like that of being comfortably filled with roast beef; love, like being enlivened with champagne.

SAMUEL JOHNSON

Love begins with love; and the warmest friendship cannot change even to the coldest love.

LA BRUYÈRE

There are no rules for friendship. It must be left to itself. We cannot force it any more than love.

WILLIAM HAZLITT

The only reward of virtue is virtue; the only way to have a friend is to be one.

RALPH WALDO EMERSON

Greater love hath no man than this, that a man lay down his life for his friends.

JOHN 15:13

I count myself in nothing else so happy
As in a soul remembering my good friends.

SHAKESPEARE,
Richard II

Friendship is one mind in two bodies.

MENCIUS

Two lovely berries moulded on one stem:
So, with two seeming bodies, but one heart.

SHAKESPEARE,
A Midsummer Night's Dream

My heart is ever at your service.

SHAKESPEARE,
Timon of Athens

It is a true saying that we must eat many measures of salt together to be able to discharge the functions of friendship.

CICERO

Keep your fears to yourself,
but share your courage with others.

ROBERT LOUIS STEVENSON

Friendship improves happiness, and abates misery, by doubling our joy, and dividing our grief.

JOSEPH ADDISON

No matter where we are we need those friends who trudge across from their neighborhoods to ours.

STEPHEN PETERS

All men have their frailties: and whoever looks for a friend without imperfections, will never find what he seeks. We love ourselves notwithstanding our faults, and we ought to love our friends in like manner.

CYRUS

Madam, I have been looking for a person who disliked gravy all my life; let us swear eternal friendship.

SYDNEY SMITH

Someone to laugh with me, someone to be grave with me, someone to please me and help my discrimination with his . . . own remark, and at times, no doubt, to admire my acuteness and penetration.

ROBERT BURNS

We can never replace a friend. When a man is fortunate enough to have several, he finds they are all different. No one has a double in friendship.

JOHANN SCHILLER

I find friendship to be like wine, raw when new, ripened with age, the true old man's milk and restorative cordial.

THOMAS JEFFERSON

If a man does not make new acquaintance as he advances through life, he will soon find himself left alone. A man, Sir, should keep his friendship in constant repair.

SAMUEL JOHNSON

All we can do is to make the best of our friends, love and cherish what is good in them, and keep out of the way of what is bad.

THOMAS JEFFERSON

I am not bound to win but I am bound to be true. I am not bound to succeed but I am bound to live up to what light I have. I must stand with anybody that stands right: stand with him while he is right and part with him when he goes wrong.

ABRAHAM LINCOLN

When friends meet, hearts warm.

PROVERB

Best friend, my well-spring in the wilderness!

GEORGE ELIOT

The most I can do for my friend is simply to be his friend. I have no wealth to bestow on him. If he knows that I am happy in loving him, he will want no other reward. Is not friendship divine in this?

HENRY DAVID THOREAU

May the hinges of friendship never rust, or the wings of luve lose a feather.

DEAN EDWARD BANNERMAN RAMSEY

A FRIEND

There is no friend like an old friend
Who has shared our morning days,
No greeting like his welcome,
No homage like his praise.
Fame is the scentless flower,
With gaudy crown of gold;
But friendship is the breathing rose,
With sweets in every fold.

OLIVER WENDELL HOLMES

THE ARROW AND THE SONG

I shot an arrow into the air,
It fell to earth, I knew not where;
For, so swiftly it flew, the sight
Could not follow it in its flight.

I breathed a song into the air,
It fell to earth, I knew not where;
For who has sight so keen and strong,
That it can follow the flight of song?

Long, long afterward, in an oak
I found the arrow, still unbroke;
And the song, from beginning to end,
I found again in the heart of a friend.

HENRY WADSWORTH LONGFELLOW

The years between
Have taught me some sweet,
Some bitter lessons; none
Wiser than this—to
Spend in all things else,
But of old friends,
Be most miserly.

JAMES RUSSELL LOWELL

TO MY FRIEND

I love you not only for what you are, but for what I am when I am with you.

I love you not only for what you have made of yourself, but for what you are making of me.

I love you because you have done more than any creed could have done to make me good, and more than any fate could have done to make me happy.

You have done it without a touch, without a word, without a sign.

You have done it by being yourself. Perhaps that is what being a friend means, after all.

ANONYMOUS